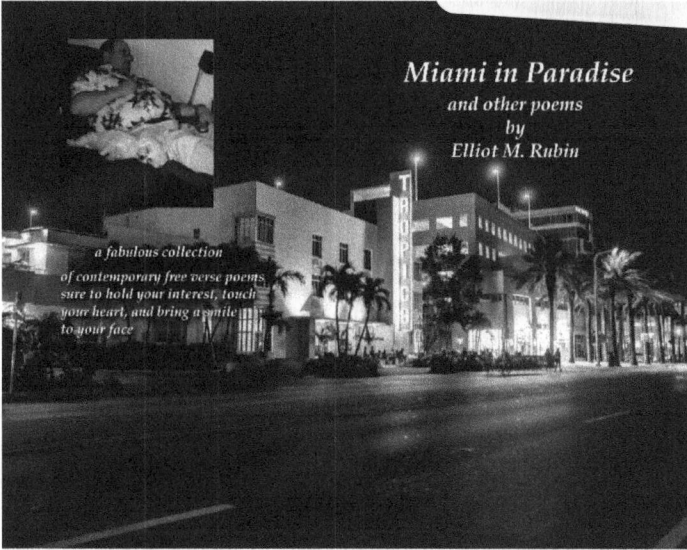

Miami in Paradise
and other poems
by
Elliot M. Rubin

a fabulous collection
of contemporary free verse poems
sure to hold your interest, touch
your heart, and bring a smile
to your face

Miami in Paradise

and other poems

cover by Ryan Spencer at Unsplash.com

Dedication
To my grandchildren
Shane, Isabelle, Jonathan, Carter,
Alexandra, Melanie, Mollie, and Madison

In memory of my father
Herman S. Rubin
who wrote poetry all his life

I believe poetry is to be read and understood by all. It needs to be written in plain language for everyone's enjoyment.

Too often, poets write in-depth, penetrating poems where you need to be well-read and/or versed in literature's nuances to appreciate the poetry, not this book or any of my writings. I try to write so everyone can enjoy a few moments of intellectual satisfaction without consulting a dictionary or encyclopedia

Table of Contents

florida

arriving in miami
cool airport
no humidity
you lose it
once you step outside;
sweltering heat
hair curls
brows sweat
body perspires
maine missed

you go from
air-conditioned home,
to air-conditioned garage,
to air-conditioned car
to air-conditioned mall,
rarely outside
where bugs the size of large mice prosper

alligators are everywhere
looking to snack on dogs, cats, or you–
first time i ever thought of myself
as a protein-rich dinner for an animal;
kind of a reverse supermarket in a way

welcome to florida

miami paradise

ocean breezes
by the beach
do not overcome
oppressive heat,
people suffer
while sunning
on blankets
under tropical sun

pink building facades
match hidden flesh tones
under burnt-umber
suntanned bodies of seniors,
who freely abandon
restrictive shackles
of religious doctrines
from their youth,
as they live a life of lust
with moral freedom
formerly denied them
by society and family,
enjoying hedonistic
lifestyles
in their remaining years

room 101 - part one

only a block from the beach,
a small, around-the-corner-hotel
caters to a select clientele
who appreciate discretion

a couple enters the dark lobby,
blinding glare of sunshine at their back
the elderly gentleman goes to register,
asks for a quiet room for the afternoon

seeing his thin skeletal hand
with bulging blue veins
scribble his name on the card,
the clerk knows the scene-
mr john smith gives a black credit card
with a different name,
the gold wedding band explains the rest

waiting for him in the lobby:
a young latina with thick, cascading black hair
wears a flashy, open pink flamingo print blouse
a skin-tight, hot pink mini skirt -
her tan, olive-skinned legs
flow down to a pair of pink,
six-inch-high stilettos

the clerk gives him room 101
a first-floor room is easier and quicker
for an ambulance crew
to get to him for resuscitation

room 101 - part two

the afternoon went fast
since the old man finished
in under an hour then left;
the room was paid for the day–
with time to kill, the latina
orders room service on his card,
then went to the hotel spa
for a naked deep tissue massage–
after, in the sauna, towel-less
she met young man
who asks her out for a drink
that evening at the rooftop bar,
after they start to kiss–
in early evening the crisp,
salty ocean breeze floats in
while Pina Coladas keep coming–
the bartender, shirtless, slender,
tries to kiss men at the bar
hello on the cheek, hoping
to get lucky for later-
the latina ends up back in 101–
in the heat of passion, the man
places his hands around her neck
squeezing hard until she pokes his
eyes, jumps out of bed, races
to her bag, pulls out a snub nose 38;
demands his Rolex plus a
diamond-encrusted ring–
blinking in pain, he complies;
then a pillow is placed over
the gun and shots are fired-
she throws everything in her bag,
closes the door,
walks away

downtown miami

in little havana
all you hear is spanish,
the smell of cigar smoke floats about,
fights the salty ocean breezes
seeking to dominate the air

handsome young men
with piercing dark eyes,
thick wavy black hair,
wearing open shirts
with skin-tight slacks
don't call out,
no need;
women are attracted
without trying–
blond dyed older women
way past prime
cozy up to them
wearing strong perfume
trying to impress,
hoping sagging jowls,
weathered skin,
chasm's of crows feet
do not deter from obtaining
an evening
of paid pleasure

miami singles

singles scene
in miami
for men
is a veritable
smorgasbord
of older widows
living out
repressed youth–
so many
to choose from,
not enough viagra
to go around;
it taxes
stamina,
too hard
on a senior man's heart

what a way to die

alone in miami

on a holiday
i am al**one**

are you aware
one is in it

i am al**one**
when the **one**
i love is g**one**

miss you

the purse

miami sun shines through a window
heating the room
she turns on air conditioning
in the condo she bought ten years ago
when she moved here with her husband

he's gone now,
                buried yesterday

few friends left
she sits alone in silence in the kitchen
nursing an ice tea with a lemon wedge,
staring in silence at the coach bag
he bought her last month as a present
for their fiftieth anniversary

now past noon, still not dressed
to start a day of nothing,
                      nowhere to go,
                      emptiness–
turns the bag on its side
to take out a crocodile skin wallet
with old family pictures inside

leafs through, she pauses at each one;
allows memories of good times to surface,
knowing today will be like tomorrow,
and the next day after too;
                  alone,
inside in her hot miami retirement condo

second honeymoon in miami

the elderly couple
flew in
from the midwest
to celebrate
their fortieth anniversary
in the same hotel room
as on their honeymoon

they with gray hair and physical ailments,
like the couple, the hotel has aged,
not shiny and sprite as years ago–
well maintained unless you look closely,
fraying corners on rugs and sofas,

after entering their room in early evening,
they undress,
shower,
gently slip into bed
pulling the covers up

unlike years ago,
this time they fall asleep

north haulover beach - miami

determined
to be like everyone else,
to fit in,
at twenty-five, she decides to go,
her friends took her there one day

here every one is naked;
fat, chubby, overweight, stocky, muscular,
thin, skinny, emaciated,
all body types can be found, ignored

they undress, placing clothes
in a bag on a corner, other stuff
 a few feet away in a pile–
stretched out on a blanket, stiff,
she is between her girlfriends

now she feels
like others on the beach,
exposed to the sun,
even with cerebral palsy
she fits in

deli

jacobson's new york style deli
is a beacon
for a genuine missed experience;
elderly waitresses call you dear,
speak with Brooklyn accents,
only place mustard or ketchup on the table,
never mayo

people line up
waiting
with no elbow space,
conversations overheard
can be joined in
while brisket or corned beef on rye is eaten,
dr. browns cel-ray soda is served,
also, with homemade knishes and sour pickles

women wear diamond rings and bracelets
that sparkle as wrists lift food
to smeared, painted red lips, full facial makeup,
in designer clothes,
                          it is only lunch

after closing, leftover food
is brought to a food bank to feed those
homeless and hungry
without diamonds

1960's La Sagüesera

years ago on Flagler Street and 12th Avenue
cubanitas serve dark Cuban coffee
in small, white porcelain cups to old men
who speak of a Cuba they fled years ago,
to start over in America

tales of their old lives
before Castro,
shared in lowered voices
when a prison is mentioned,
harsh stories retold, torture, people killed;
old habits are hard to leave behind

Fernando puffs on a fresh, hand-rolled cigar
as he adjusts a straw hat with a thin black fabric
run around the brim, the same style he wore
before he was arrested
by la policia in a cantina
for speaking things, years ago, in Viñales

the years he spent as a young man
rolling cigars with his father are remembered,
while he watches in the window of a cigar store
as wet, brown-stained fingers roll tobacco

Latin music blares into the street,
Criollo cooking, Cuban sandwiches,
are available in newly opened restaurants
serving an old culture, alive in Miami,
with memories, longing to return
handed down to children

sadly,
once Americanized, they may not care

tickets

he never had season tickets,
then he moved to miami–
the team he followed
religiously this year
is in the super bowl

living on retirement income
he couldn't afford a ticket
so applied for a job at the
stadium hoping to see it live

the day of the game,
ready to leave for work
sharp pain in his foot
stopped his walking

he had to watch
the game on tv,
gout doesn't care

domino park

the squares on the floor
are a mix of black and white,
while concrete tables rest on it–
crowds stand around
under palm trees
to watch the intense games.
played with a serious zeal
not unlike a soccer match
reeking with machismo

the cuban men
smoke and play
a quick game–
banter is heard back and forth,
nonstop talk in spanish,
yet ignored by the payers
with cigars hanging from their lips–

snap, snap
dominoes tap
on the tables,
wrists twist them down
with white dots face up

only members
of the club
are allowed to play,
while a stray dog
stretches out
in the shade
for a siesta,
ignoring them

swamp prodigy

born in the backwaters
of rural florida
seems normal
looking at him,
but his brain
works differently

he can name
all sixty-seven
of the state's counties
in alphabetical order,
even backward,
if asked

never forgets,
reads it once
never forgets,
hears it once,
some say brilliant–
can't relate to others
can't make a living

lives with swamp people

reading in miami

in self-quarantine she
ignores the governor
who drank GOP kool-aid

virus rages,
some stores closed,
won't go shopping
or even to browse

locked at home
she reads all-day
looks for old friends
in the daily obits—
it's time for her
to get a new hobby

left the cold for miami

left new york
it is too cold—
my miami home is heated
when winter comes-
my down comforter
keeps me warm, yet
i need to wear socks
when i go to bed;
seems i have
summer feet
that always freeze

silent wish

tomorrow her daughter
will be married-
she sits on her bed
in a pink nightgown
with small blue flowers,
sadly
her parents are still in cuba—
they never lived the life she does,
there was no space on the boat,
just enough for their daughter;
they paid for her to leave

tears of sadness
mix with heartache;
for tomorrow
a new free family
begins now in miami

unsaid
a silent wish
is for her daughter
to someday
visit grandparents
in a free cuba

amsterdam in miami

on her way to work
in the red light district
she stops to purchase
her bags of
sativa or indicia,
depends
on her schedule,
who she will be with
tonight

when she returns home
early morning
she will decide
which one
to roll,
smoke,
chill out with–
life is not easy
when you have
to make a living
faking love;
seems similar
to her marriage

pride parade

standing on the sidewalk
i watch marchers
in colorful,
skimpy,
in some cases
almost nonexistent costumes
pass in front of me

marcher's laughter,
their wide smiles
bring levity to the area
as bars emptied
to watch,
cheer them on,
while the smell
of marijuana hangs
in a cloud
above the parade

every combination
of lovers
walk hand in hand,
kissing strangers,
bystanders,
proving
there is no such thing
as bad love

miami sins

the heat is unbearable;
 black asphalt radiates it back up,
sweat never stops
 it floods my clothes;
beads form all over my body,
 it's impossible to cool down

is this a city from hell?
 what sins did everyone do?

if so…
 then i missed out
  on the fun

spring break/first time

nineteen,
she drove to miami beach with friends
to sun on the sand,
dance at clubs
drink with boys
'til matchups go back to motel rooms

not pretzel stick thin,
her bikini barely covers,
attracting company to
sit on her towel
every morning before noon
as the sun rises on the horizon

a young man she drank with last night
asked if he could slather on suntan lotion

gently
  he rubs her back
   then shoulders,
when she turns over
he applies it to her stomach;
  soft circles,
   a light rotating touch
    then lower,
     lower,
      gliding over forbidden fruit
finding treasure with no objections

Other Poems

essential

divorced
  single mother,
every morning
  when she leaves
  to work in a hospital,
says goodbye to
the dog and two daughters

hazmat suit
  head to toes
holding a phone
  for families to view
    dying loved ones,
then in a gloved hand
 holds theirs
    as they enter
their final sleep

after administrators
  get theirs first,
she waits days
  for her vaccine

sitting at the curb

once knew a guy
with a bright smile
down on his luck

he gambles
  wages away,
lives in moms basement,
  only small hits
    waiting for a big one
while his car is repossessed,
his wife left with the kid,
stressed out
  hit bottom but didn't lookup–
never went to meetings,
just a matter of time
  till he can't pay his bets;
    the bookies want their cash
      don't wait forever

broken bones do heal,
if he survives

marriage

some say marriage
is a 50/50 arrangement,
i think it should be
more a 100/100 deal;
  you are all in on it
or not

there will be days
either one
ticks the other off,
  sometimes royally–
you need to want
to grow old together,
  for forever

work out aggravations
with the intention
the last person
  you are with
    on your final day on earth
will be your life partner;
  saying

i love you

one last time

intolerance

because a person
is not white skinned,
  their religion is not christian,
    or people of the same sex
      who love each other,
or those with mental issues
  are discriminated against,
or folks struggling to survive
  are looked down at

republicans don't care

finally, we are at the end of the national trump era
finally, we are at the end of the national trump error

maybe the healing can begin

nyu - washington square 1964

springtime, after morning class,
going to the park to hang out–
a hippie chick in the school hallway
grabs my hand,
"let's go to the fountain," she said,
not asking, so we went

long, straight, brown hair
dressed in a madras print dress
multi stained, hippie wooden love beads
around her neck;
    we never met before

the park is busy,
people smoking weed,
a guy on a milk box talks about
overthrowing government,
one preaches repentance while
a bleached blond girl
with a tight blouse, hands out flyers
for a late-night student bar/hangout–
the fountain gushes next to us
when she puts her hands around my neck
pulls me close, we kiss;
  free love is in the air;
    we walk arm in arm to her dorm room

opposites attract, i guess,
or we were both horny,
  it didn't matter

susan is a city girl,
midtown private girls schools,
well educated enjoys her college freedoms–

i grew up in brooklyn,
public education,
wanted to be a musician,
not go to college, not be a lawyer;
life has twists and turns

not every young romance lasts;
after a few months, she left on a freedom bus
to register voters in the south–
a quick decision, she said goodbye

i never saw her again
    except in my dreams

cecilia

i can't say her name anymore–
i use to spill it out with ease,
it was a song on my tongue
with love on my lips

the rain stops,
it covers black, dark asphalt
with a glistening sheen
filling potholes,
reflecting trees
as i walk along–
the sun shining
bright,
a cheerful day now

yet i am despondent

breakups are hard
when they come;
love is forever

someone never told her

busy

i'm busy
writing,
posting,
publishing books
because at seventy-five
tomorrow is not promised;
i only have today
to get my voice
down in print

aged 20 years

take a swig
  of single malt whisky,
feel the warmth
feel the heat below

taste the smoked barrel's
  fermented delight,
the strength of the liquor
  aged twenty years

amber brewed,
  it swishes as it flows,
not unlike
  the full-bodied young girl,
who gently
  pours it out for me,
as i wait
  to savor them both

a day in infamy #2

a shot rang out—
the rioter fell dead
wrapped in trump flags
in a capital hallway

windows smashed,
congress stopped,
the instigator in hiding
secured blocks away

treason is serious,
punishment severe,
he deserves
a mussolini ending

reaching up

young,
long flowing hair,
tall,
slender legs,
shapely body,
pretty face,
beyond what he should attain

i don't understand?

why would
she want
an old,
bald,
overweight,
sickly,
wealthy man

disappointment on instagram

her small picture shows
a pretty blond woman
with full red lips—
she followed me

it was a private account
so i followed back
to see what she writes—
i get a one-word response

hi!

i answer back *hi*

would i like to make
thousands of dollars?
she wrote to me

depends, i answer,

she wanted me to send her money
if i wanted to see her privately at home

it was another cash scam

needless to say
i am disappointed

i thought she wanted **my** body

caught

business as usual
nothing different,
until her lover
overstayed

suddenly her
husband is home
                    too soon

dog barking
door opening
dress quickly
dash to the closet
                    the priest hides

a capital officer's goodbye

the casket
is set in front,
covered
with the flag of the nation
as mourners walk in
to pay their respects

after the chaplain
finishes prayers
the widow
is escorted
out of her seat
to walk
to her husband's
flag-draped casket

tears drip as she bends
to kiss
the red, white, and blue fabric,
rests her cheek for a lingering moment,
then goes back to her seat

the instigator of the insurrection
never shows up

January 6th

hang mike pence, hang mike pence

the seditious mob's chants echo
  in the capital's hallways–
chaos
mayhem
unbridled anger

few against the mob
   officers beaten back
    physically abused
      overwhelmed
        death happens

capital police
undermanned
under-managed
abandoned
  by the president

a fate similar to
the charge of the light brigade

not forgotten,
  honored for bravery

a puritan society

the line running up
    the back of her leg
is a thin black tattoo,
    not a silk seam

it would end with a lace panty
    under a short skirt
if you looked,
    except it isn't there

she works in a house
    but doesn't do housework–
her skill is faux marital bliss
    to those who pay enough

man or woman
    doesn't matter,
it's a job
    though not 9 to 5–
a marriage license
    makes it legal
for doing
    the exact same work

horses

two summers ago
i went to the racetrack
for a food truck festival with
nine thoroughbred races

in one of the races
on the far turn
one horse fell,
trucks came out,
a curtain is raised
then a loud gunshot

this worried me
when i tripped at home,
broke my right femur–
my wife had a strange look
on her face at that moment

christmas memories

she remembers as a child
father brought her to town
to see the holiday lights
strung across streets from
light posts and buildings
for the holiday season–
mother had her help hang
decorations, and trim the
real tree father fresh cut–
as a young bride, the future
looked so bright until it didn't–
the blackness descended,
her world turned dark, the
wedding vows broke with
the pills and drink–
now in manhattan, she sleeps
in a cardboard box on top
of subway sidewalk grates
for warmth, remembering
yesterdays as hundreds of
different feet walk by,
she is invisible
to them as they
celebrate the holiday

kool-aid

dear leaders
 mixed the powder,
their media
 fed it to them,
almost half the nation
 drank it,
they believed every drop

lies,
half-truths
alternate facts,
mistrust others,
  only his words
    are what is right

zombie people
  ignore
    everyone else,
they
    drank the kool-aid–
brought jonestown to america

writing poetry

poetry is a means
of communication,
to tell a story,
a feeling, evoke emotion

some poets try to impress others
with polysyllabic or esoteric words;
force us to use a dictionary
to try to understand them

i believe the best way
to communicate with words
is to use simple, easy ones,
you literati elitist snob

who you really are

all the mirrors
in the house are covered;
they reflect your image
every time i look

don't want them cracked,
 i see you in them–
the veins in the glass
remind me
of your drained heart,
hardly beating,
took what you could,
cheating,
lies,
immune to feeling love,
i thought you were the summer heat
  in my heart

i was wrong,
  you're the ice storm of winter

still primitive

the inca's stone pyramids
were a sacrificial platform
to satiate the gods
for good crops, rain,
and punish losers
of sports games

black asphalt streets
stain red with the blood
of our youth, the
losers in a society
of racists intent on
supporting wealth
instead of the struggling

young virgin girls
were tossed in volcanoes
to appease the gods
ending drought,
guarantee tribal success

today young women are
forced to sacrifice bodies
for opiates to feed a habit,
paying pimps, or dancing nude
in a hypocritical evangelical society
that ignores the plight
of the unprivileged
to satiate the rich,
who impose
their moral values on others

domestic abuse

bruises tell a tale
blueblack, pain left days ago
memories last years

walk past

amazing how we see
   yet are blind
to others troubles
when it's not our problem

people don't realize
in the end,
their issues
are ours, too

homelessness
hunger
hate—
harbingers of

humanity's ills
eventually
come home
to haunt us

your tongue

behind pretty red lips,
which when pursed
inspire delightful thoughts,
lies a flexible body part

some say you need it
to help chew,
taste food,
make love

i think its primary function
is to enable
orgasmic delight,
when your tongue
touches chocolate

bud

a mall store is selling
a fire engine red leather jacket
with the budweiser logo on the back;
for a moment, i consider a purchase

then realize
i'd need a motorcycle too,
also a young mistress
with no moral scruples

a pied a terre for us to meet,
furnish it with a round bed,
mirror the ceiling,
go to the gym
    to keep in shape

although everything
sounds great in my mind
i then kept walking

too much effort
    just to buy a jacket

vail, colorado

a winter playground
to ski all day
dance all night
breathe fresh air

the ski lift in summer
takes you to the top
where you can bike
downhill, or just look around

in vail, i first tasted
a new type of filet mignon
my palate never experienced,
or will ever again

too expensive,
too gamey,
too small a cut,
venison is not my thing

too thin

looking back
at teenage years
the bedroom mirror
enabled me
to count ribs,
all of them,
i saw myself as heavy

it took years
to gain weight,
to fill out
as mom used to call it,
not realizing until weight watchers
asked why i want to join

my truthful answer
shocked them,
i told them
i am a recovering
anorexic–
in adulthood
i discovered food;
my ribs are now well hidden

donald

he built
buildings,
fancy,
glitzy,
ornate,
admired others too
except for one
towering
high above the others

the empire state building
is very tall–
psychologists said
he couldn't look at it
due to penis envy

deja vu

every day is tomorrow again
meeting new friends
tasting foods for the first time
feeling love with smiles

doesn't matter
that yesterday
is the same as today
or tomorrow is the same

dementia doesn't distinguish

I want to thank
my Friday poetry critique group
for their help in editing my poetry.
Bill, Carol, David, Jill,
Rodney, Sue, Asha, Rich,

the end

www.CreativeFiction.net
for of all my books